COMMENTS FROM READERS

"*Meditation: Waking Up to Life* draws from a lifetime of reflection and practice, and it shows. In page after page of thought-provoking observations and lyrical passages, Americ Azevedo invites the reader to set out upon, or perhaps re-di~~~~ ~~~~ journey toward profound unde~~~~ ~~~~ding and peace ~~~~ ~~~~ ~~~~ and with the world."

—Jerry Sanders, C~~~~ ~~~~ Peace~~~~ ~~~~ ~~~~ ~~~~ U~~~~ ~~~~ ~~~~ ~~~~, Berkeley

———————

"The tone of the book is so inviting, and I think it will be of great value to people who have a meditation practice, and to those who have never meditated. The book collects stories, aphorisms, poems, reflections, and presents them unpretentiously, so that the reader can open to any page and just sit and reflect on Azevedo's words, inviting a deep look into our own beings and our lives. The book distills the wisdom of a lifetime as a teacher, a meditator, and a person of deep spirit. It is a call to waking up, to being fully present in each moment."

—Charles Halpern, Chair and Co-Founder,
Center for Contemplative Mind in Society
Author of *Making Waves and Riding the Currents:*
Activism and the Practice of Wisdom

———

"On the first day of class Professor Azevedo said that 'meditation is nothing' and that 'meditation cannot be taught.' The simplicity of his introduction seemed only to verify the rumors that PACS 94: Theory and Practice of Meditation would be 'the easiest class you'll ever take.' I soon came to realize that my quest to understand reality would be the most difficult and important journey that I would ever make in my lifetime.

"Upon learning that 'meditation is nothing,' the human mind rushes to make sense of something which makes no sense whatsoever. It subconsciously constructs its own definition of 'the nothingness which is meditation.'

"Concept by concept, Professor Azevedo's book teaches us to let go of bits and pieces of this construct so that we can move closer to accepting the simple and pure 'nothingness which is meditation.'

"The book, therefore, does not claim to teach meditation, but serves as an invaluable, life-long reminder of my commitment to being aware (HERE, NOW) and to understanding absolute reality. It comes directly from the heart. The book is not a continuous manual, but a collection of improvised passages, thereby leaving room for contemplation and experimentation."

—Aria Pakatchi, First Year,
Intended Molecular Cell Biology major
University of California, Berkeley

"Americ Azevedo is 'not your average academic philosopher'. He has spent years in the gritty end of business: working in the IT operation of a big oil company, for example. He has been entrepreneurial all his life, with his own Goldwarp consulting operation. He pioneered early distance learning concepts for an important business-oriented university. It has been a pleasure to be with him on collaborative calls at giants of industry such as Hewlett Packard. Most recently he has provided unique leadership in learning, and life, to students across three diverse disciplines at UC Berkeley. In *Meditation, Waking Up to Life*, Americ once again provides us with a perspective which is both spiritual and uplifting, and grounded as a good business plan."

—Terry Pettengill, President,
OCULUS Management Process, Inc.,
Business Consultants in Strategy,
Innovation and Communication
Mill Valley, California

"I tried meditation many years ago, and got little out of it. While I do not endorse meditation, if you must try it out for yourself, your best help will be this little booklet."

—Mark Rubinstein, Finance Professor
University of California, Berkeley

MEDITATION

Waking Up to Life

Americ Azevedo

University of California, Berkeley

San Diego, CA

First published in the United States of America in 2010 by Cognella, a division of University Readers, Inc.

14 13 12 11 10   1 2 3 4 5

Printed in the United States of America

ISBN: 978-1-935551-03-4

www.cognella.com 800.200.3908

To Glenn Matson

*For years of daily focus
on meditation and peace of mind.*

ACKNOWLEDGMENTS

This work is derived from working with the amazing students of PACS 94 "Theory and Practice of Meditation" at the University of California, Berkeley. Fearlessly facing the truths of life, they give me hope for a nonviolent, enlightened world in the future.

I wish to express my appreciation to Jerry Sanders, Chair, Peace and Conflict Studies, for the opportunity to teach the class; and to Michael Nagler for his vision in initiating this meditation course at U.C. Berkeley.

Also thanks to followers of my online meditation posts, and to the wonderful people who have participated in my Meditation Mini-Retreats and TeleWisdom telephone conference calls.

Special thanks to Athena Azevedo, my daughter, for exceptionally strong encouragement, and for the cover photographs. Thanks to Marianne Henry for reading and commenting on the first draft, and her many suggestions. And, thanks to Melissa Accornero, Acquisitions Editor, and all the patient staff at University Readers/Cognella, for moving this book into production and publication.

Also, I must honor my father, Frank Azevedo. He taught me the value of a personal spiritual connection while I was still a little child. Those seeds planted, have grown into a garden.

Finally, of course, my great appreciation to Diane Shavelson, my life partner, for content improvements, editing, and her overall encouragement and support, without which this work would not have been possible.

Contents

Preface

Reflecting back, I realize that I have been meditating as long as I can remember. As a young child, I would sit and stare at the clock, still enough to see the hands move. As I walked home from school, I would see, if for a whole block, I could concentrate on the sidewalk without a distracting thought. At sunset I loved to sit and focus 100 percent of my attention on watching the changing light.

Perhaps my formal meditation practice began in 1971, while teaching my first course, "Mysticism and Science," at San Francisco State University. As I talked of mysticism, a student challenged me to explore meditation. I began by exploring the practices and philosophies of Maharishi Mahesh Yogi and Chögyam Trungpa. Over the years I encountered many other teachers, and, as always, continued as a student of everyday life; all of this informing my practice and my investigation of mind, as I evolved into a practice and philosophy that is uniquely my own.

———

When I teach meditation, I make the point that no particular religion or metaphysics is needed for meditation—just moving the mind state from distraction to attention. Doing this, for even just a short time, improves life in unexpected ways.

———

This book is made up of 108 teachings—the number of beads in Buddhist and Hindu meditation beads; which are divided into nine sections. The "beads" are in no special order. They are intended to inspire meditation practice; not necessarily theorize. There is plenty of empty page space. Write notes in it. Make it your own.

May these small nuggets support your meditation practice, whether beginner, intermediate, or advanced. We are all beginners on many paths of meditation—be it our first day or our fortieth year of practice. May our practice inform all of life. May we awaken to life here-and-now.

One

All this is full. All that is full.
From fullness, fullness comes.
When fullness is taken from fullness,
Fullness still remains.

—THE UPANISHADS

Invitation to Meditation

Every time, every moment is a good time to meditate. Why wait for a retreat or some special time or place? Why not just take a minute right now. Yes, it's always time to meditate. The ultimate root of procrastination is the tendency to postpone the encounter with this present moment. Actually, to avoid meditation is to avoid life. To meditate is to face life, to awaken to life. Life can only be lived here-and-now, not there-and-then.

Beyond Philosophy

A lover of wisdom may speak of wisdom all day long, yet not live that wisdom. Someone who possesses wisdom may say nothing wise at all.

As a graduate student in philosophy, I became frustrated with philosophy itself. I saw academic philosophy as a craft without real answers to my deepest concerns. T. S. Elliot's lines from "The Rock" moved my soul:

> The endless cycle of idea and action,
> Endless invention, endless experiment,
> Brings knowledge of motion, but not stillness;
> Knowledge of speech, but not of silence;
> Knowledge of words and ignorance of the Word.
> . . . .
> Where is the Life we have lost in living?
> Where is the wisdom we have lost in knowledge?
> Where is the knowledge we have lost information?

Shortly thereafter, Chögyam Trungpa showed up as a classroom guest speaker. He wore a blazer and turtle neck shirt, holding a can of Coca-Cola in his hand—not my image of an Eastern guru or yogi. He spoke directly and spontaneously. It took many years to realize that his presence was the teaching more than his words. Now, I don't remember the words, but the presence remains. I look, and feel, for that same presence in others and within myself.

Our Work Is to Awaken

Our work, our labor, is to awaken to our true nature, which was forgotten due to false identification with the content of consciousness.

The theory and practice of meditation help us realize (make real) our true nature. When I speak, write or listen to these words, I am often in the realm of theory. When I take in the meaning of these words, I inform and transform myself along the path of self realization.

It is very, very important to remember that words are not what they refer to. "The map is not the territory." Speaking or writing about meditation is not meditation. Meditation is in the gaps between the words, between the thoughts. But the word "gap" is not the same as a gap itself, as it is. Get past the words—allow the great silence to come. At the point of great silence is the great labor of liberation.

Unrealized True Wealth

We are born with true wealth, but constantly forget to realize the wealth we already have. Failing to acknowledge our true wealth we keep grasping for more, like hungry ghosts who are never satisfied while constantly eating! Thus, we go about despoiling the earth, corrupting relationships, and twisting societies into grotesque forms that promote needless suffering for ourselves, others, and the earth as a whole. Realizing true wealth leads to personal, interpersonal, and transpersonal fulfillment. Furthermore, the long-term survival of life on earth depends upon true wealth realization.

We need deep psychological and spiritual healing of individuals, groups, communities, nations, and the earth. The bedrock of this healing is a return to this present moment, not in a selfish, narrow way, but in a way that includes the totality of what is here–there as well as what is in the past–present–future. It is nothing less than the ancient ideal of enlightenment of all sentient beings.

Beyond Objects

The purpose of true meditation is to break the mind's identification with objects, so that the mind simply turns toward the source—light of awareness without object. This is the spacious, sky-like, radiant quality of mind that we glimpse and sustain as we awaken; like "being in love" when the whole world seems brighter, more real, more filled with love all around. The difference is that this awakened condition is not dependent upon any object or specific person. It just IS.

Beyond Death

Is death real?

We don't die, we transform. The ego is the space-time point where future and past meet. At death or unconsciousness, that space-time point that we call "I" disappears. But, the real Self which sustained us all along does not die, it continues as the rest of all-that-is.

This great "secret" resides in the depths explored through meditation.

Gaps Are Openings to Deep Reality

Meditation creates "gaps" in our mental reality. These gaps are gifts.

When an important part of life falls apart, a gap is created. That gap is the opportunity to allow in deep reality. If we close that gap too quickly, old familiar patterns snap back into place. Stay with a gap just long enough to realize that it's a gift, an opportunity for awakening.

We don't need to have our lives fall apart to experience the benefits of gaps—in meditation we sit and allow ourselves to be aware of gaps as they come. This is deliberate and less dramatic but the results can be more dramatic in the fullness of time.

Each Thought Dies Peacefully Away

When successive thoughts do not await one another, and each thought dies peacefully away, this is called absorption in the oceanic reflection.

—Zen Master Mazu

During meditation, notice that thoughts breed thoughts. One thought follows another for a while in a chain of free association. There will be days when only a few related thoughts come. On other days, hundreds of related thoughts march on, one after the other, building up entire stories of their own making—so it seems. With vigilance, we can release these thoughts from the quality of "awaiting one another." They, die peacefully away. The sense of open, oceanic stillness suddenly arrives.

Drop by Drop

Don't worry about "getting there" immediately. Quick fixes don't work. Patience is a critical part of "progress." So, relax, and enjoy the journey.

Water erodes mountains,
bit by bit, drop by drop,
carving out whole valleys.

"No such thing as an overnight success";
Behind every successful
performer, writer, businessman,
there are years of hard work, practice,
and failure.

Life is practice; practice is life.
Practice receiving; practice letting go.
Practice deciding when to do something
Rather than letting circumstances decide.

Don't think all or nothing;
do something anyway.
Small daily investments in practice
grow "spiritual principle" over a lifetime.

Mind Waves

Mind freely associates from thought to thought; without discipline, constantly surfing the edge of reality.

Waves of thoughts keep coming, an endless stream of mental associations. We learn from some texts and living teachers that the mind must be disciplined or controlled in some way; but, this is not quite it. If a controlled mind is all we are seeking, then meditation becomes an isolated act divorced from life; a way of escape.

It's not the thoughts themselves that must go, but the ego that uses this ocean of thoughts to create separation from reality.

Effortless Desires

*A radio receiver tunes into a frequency in the air; in that sense,
something in the radio matches what is out there.*

We effortlessly desire
truth, beauty, and *wisdom*
because our souls are made of
truth, beauty, and wisdom.
The deep charm of meditation
is that it opens
doors to the soul.

Everyone Is "Me"

Everyone else is "me." That's the basis of the "Golden Rule."

Everywhere we go we
run up against *others.*
Everyone of them is "me" or
"I."
Clearly,
"we" are all one.
By cultivating spiritual eyes we
see this.

Two

Move like a beam of light:
Fly like lightning,
Strike like thunder,
Whirl in circles around
a stable center.

—MORIHEI UESHIBA[1]

---

1 Founder of the Aikido martial art.

Living in the In-between

A flower grows between sidewalk cracks. A smile shines between tears. A life unfolds between birth and death.

We often want things all firmed up and tidy. We want sidewalks to be sidewalks, smiles to be smiles, and life to go on forever. The truth is that everything is constantly changing. Every present moment is between this and that. If you study physics you have to also know calculus—the mathematics of change. We cannot talk about the world without dealing with movement and change. Everything is in-between.

When we meditate we watch thoughts pass by; learning to always let them go. One may deepen meditation by looking for the gaps between thoughts. Pay attention to the gaps, and relax—they are glimpses of liberation.

Edge of the Abyss

We live on the edge of an abyss. There's no bottom to our minds and souls. Awareness is limitless and space-like.

We live on the edge of an abyss. The abyss of endless outer space is just above; it's the sky. The whole earth is falling into the sun, but centripetal forces push the earth out toward endless empty space. We could either freeze or fry; but, a delicate balance of forces keeps the Earth in orbit around the sun. There's no bottom to our minds and souls. Awareness is limitless and space-like. At any moment a thought, feeling or experience can fill up our minds right now. Our limitless mirror-like awareness gets filled with objects, thoughts, persons, moods, and issues. Too empty inside, we may go "nuts"; too much activity, we lose our sanity.

The confrontation with nothingness is fearsome. You cannot drop into silence and remain silent for long; silence automatically brings up anxiety. Almost immediately, we feel compelled to return to inner and outer chatter and distractions. Heidegger notes, "Anxiety robs us of speech. ... That in the malaise of anxiety, we often try to shatter the vacant stillness with compulsive talk only proves the presence of the nothing."[2]

The way to deal with nothingness is to stay with it; don't run away. Don't postpone the encounter. Feel your feet, breath deeply, keep walking through the valley of nothingness. Make deep friends with yourself; eventually the light at the end of the tunnel comes. Eventually there comes an opening to That-Which-Is—a feeling of finally being at home, right here and now.

2 *What is Metaphysics?*

Be a Spiritual Scientist

Go deep and find your own understanding.

Wisdom is not in books, speeches or web pages!
    It's in us
    Look within—
    See the universe unfolding around and within

The body-mind-spirit
    Reflects the whole cosmos

Find your own understanding
    Test it yourself
    Make sure it's true
    Be a spiritual scientist!

We Need Meditation

Because we have consciousness, we need meditation.

Life is complex and full of contradictions. We have desires. We have frustration and suffering. We have conflict. Because life is complex, we need to get to the root of life. The root of our life is consciousness.

Within meditation we simplify life to a single moment. Complexity dissolves into the clear light of consciousness.

Contemplating Words of Great Teachers

Contemplating the words of great spiritual teachers helps settle us down to meditation.

I find great power in reading the words of Moses, Jesus, Buddha, Krishna, Lao Tzu, Mohammed, and others. Suddenly my mind becomes quieter; suddenly, I feel the great Presence that is within and without. From that feeling it is often easier to sit and meditate or pray.

Mind-states

A day in the rose garden
with my daughter.
Happy just to hear
the wind, the birds,
children in the leaves.

The natural blissful human condition—the one you had as a baby—is called *sat-chit-ananda* or existence-consciousness-bliss. In ordinary life, the natural state of consciousness is covered by layers of suffering and bondage.

Falling into despair, we need to take time for prayer and meditation, but this is difficult because media, school, work, family, and general society don't have much place for soul work. The world is spiritually bankrupt.

A single day is an endless parade of ever-changing mind states, like the weather. Coffee, tea, alcohol, drugs, entertainment, or even exercise, are used to induce certain mind-states. Even a glance from a passerby on the street may change your mind-state.

States of mind are easily transmitted from person to person. The states of mind we cultivate are a great responsibility. Do not be unconscious about this. Awaken to the power you already have. Ethics begins with responsibility for our own state of mind. To have peace out in the world, you need peace in yourself; which is to spend time in *sat-chit-ananda* everyday, as often as possible.

First ...

... Undo old habits
   with focus and awareness

Everyday
so many things to do
Everyday
   my calendar fills up
I say to myself
   "I will meditate, pray, feed the spirit, too"
But there's so much to do first!

Spirit gets pushed to the bottom of the list
Life passes by
God can wait
   I have worlds to conquer

But the day goes better
when consciousness
is first on the to-do list.

Living Meditation

Meditation practices mature into "living meditation" as the fruits of practice spill over into the whole life. It's no longer practice, but life. All life becomes meditation; we become present to all life.

Brain and body move together, while mind is still. You move your hands and they are where they are, not ahead or behind where they are. It's waiting without waiting; hoping without hoping. All is as it is.

Wisdom of Imperfection

Sometimes I have heard people say to their children, "If you can't do it right, don't do it at all." This is a dangerous philosophy, for we always begin with an approximation of what we want to do. To get something "right" we have to do it "somewhat right" or "almost right." In fact, sometimes, doing it "right" might not be the best thing after all. In the imperfection of efforts there may also be the seeds of greater perfections; seeds of learning that may lead us to totally new and valued efforts.

Today's Destiny

Today! You have an appointment with destiny.

The idea of destiny suggests some future great event that must happen. For a young person, perhaps it is the day of meeting the love of their life; for a mature person, the birth of a grandchild. Destiny, however, is nothing greater than the meeting of the present with the future. When does that happen? That's when the future becomes now—today.

We can't assume some big event is going to make life "happy ever after"; but, feeling totally present today, *is* the big event.

Infinity's Window

To realize how finite we are is the window to infinity.

Jesus suggested that the meek will inherit the earth. In Islam, the daily practice of surrender is the key to true spiritual practice—indeed the word "Islam" means "surrender." We surrender to God in order to be at one with God—which is infinity personified.

But, you don't need to be religious to benefit from realizing finitude. To realize our own limitations is a great relief, because we are no longer fighting against reality but working with, going with, reality itself.

Sailing Through Life

We sail on the Sea of Life.

Sailors must know their location, time of day, and the winds and undercurrents. Living life is sailing. Our location is our body and mind states. Our time of day is our age, season of our life. All around us are winds and undercurrents, the circumstances of our lives.

But the sailor is not location, not time nor winds. The sailor is awakened consciousness, the Self itself.

Three

*Of ten thousand men, perhaps
one man strives for perfection;
Of ten thousand who strive, perhaps
one man knows me in truth.*

—BHAGAVAD GITA

Touching the Now

Now is the true point of power.

Our greatest loss
    is a loss of this present moment;
    if we are here and there
    and not all here,
    we are divided from ourselves.
    "A man cannot serve two masters," Jesus said.
    Suffering grows and power diminishes.

Ngeton said,
    "Now is the point of power!"

Fruits of the past,
    seeds of the future.

It's now—we reap past fruits,
It's now—we plant future's seeds.
    It's now—past perspectives can be changed,
    It's now—the future begins.
    Life unfolds now and now and now.

Every moment is a new beginning.

Practice Anytime

When should we practice? Anytime during the day is good. "Practice" eventually becomes all of life.

The main thing is to stay mindful. Don't get caught up in the speed of the technology age; stay at the center within—which is still and timeless.

I practice at all odd moments and hours—sometimes short, sometime long. The "practice" has evolved into many forms—yes, even while talking to friends can be "practice."

No End to Acquiring Knowledge

There's no end to acquiring knowledge of things and people; but, wisdom discerns THAT which brings rest and simple joy to the heart-mind.

When I was young, I believed that if I could read fast enough I would know everything. I learned to do speed reading; but the supply of knowledge constantly outpaced me. Eventually, I became tired and frustrated by my own project of acquiring knowledge.

In truth there's no end to acquiring knowledge of things and people. Eventually we need to stop and rise above just knowing more and more. This is when wisdom comes in. Wisdom is a level beyond knowledge. We come to understand that there's no end to acquiring knowledge of things and people; but wisdom discerns *that* which brings rest and joy to the heart-mind.

Today ... Be Silent ...

Today ... be silent ... let go, let it be—a time for cleanup of our inner and outer life.

Some of the greatest Zen masters were cooks and janitors. Some of our best days are when we do cleaning up; moving around from thing to thing, cleaning, sorting out, and putting everything away in its place. At the end of the day, you look around and feel happy with the sense of clean, clear spaciousness all around.

Good Meditation;
Bad Meditation

Don't judge yourself, just as you don't judge others. It's not about having a "good" or "bad" meditation. Get down to meditation again and again. Results take care of themselves.

Good and bad meditation sessions are of equal value. Don't worry at all about stopping the flow of thoughts. Just let them come and go as they will.

I find that a difficult meditation session filled with disturbing thoughts is in a way more powerful than a blissful session; it is a great training in patience, persistence, and perseverance. We become stronger by dealing with this the so called "bad" side of meditation.

Waterfall

In *Zen Mind, Beginner's Mind*, Suzuki gives a wonderful metaphor for life, birth, and death—a waterfall.

Picture a river flowing downstream. When the river reaches the edge of a waterfall, it breaks up into billions of drops of water. An individual life is like one of those drops. Our friends and family are the drops of water around us, that fall with us. We see ourselves as separate individuals. But at the bottom of the waterfall, we become the river again.

Life happens between the top and the bottom of the waterfall. Birth is the moment we become separate; the span of a life is the time we fall as individual drops of water; and death is the moment we merge back together.

Unity before birth, separation during life, and unity at death again.

Exercise

Imagine …
>   The thoughts
>   God would have …

You don't have to be a believer in God, just
imagine "thinking like God."

Think the thoughts that God thinks:
All is one
No separation
No grievances
No fear
No worry.

You "know" these thoughts already—
They are simple, unassuming, gentle,
True thoughts.

Woodland Walks

When life is overwhelming
I go to the woods.
There's a place in Mill Valley
—a walk that takes about half an hour
and ends at a waterfall.
Here I can smell the forest
and the ocean.

Walking here is like
shedding layers of clothes,
shedding cares of life,
slipping, falling, surrendering
to meditation.

I feel revived, cleansed, new,
A sense of unity
where self and Universe become one;
Did the Universe create me
or did I create the Universe?
Just so, Just this.

I can have the same experience in my own room,
a quiet place;
I let myself settle down
and fall into the present.

The Last Cup

We never know when "the end" comes; prepare now.

Sit with a friend and have a cup of tea;
    Imagine that this is the last cup of tea,
    Keep bringing your attention back to this situation—
    Being here at this table with this "last" cup.

Seek to feel all there is to feel about this, here and now;
    You may feel a release into the present,
    You may feel joy, or grief and loss.

The more we appreciate that
               this is the last cup,
   the closer we come to seeing that
               this is the first cup!

Root of the World

Consciousness is the root of the world. Go to the root.

Your world depends on consciousness. When you sleep in dreamless sleep, there is no world; when you awake from dreamless sleep, the world returns.

Meditation is the act of turning attention away from the world back to the source of the world as consciousness. In this sense, consciousness is the root of the world.

Mind is the limiter, the qualifier of consciousness. Consciousness is like an open cloudless sky, but mind constantly wants to put "things, moods, ideas, fantasies" into that open sky. Beyond consciousness there is awareness—a step beyond mind and consciousness—the supreme knowledge. If we go to the root of life, we live consciously. At the root there is peace and love; at the root fear constantly drops away.

Life is a Short Story

Life is over before you know it. Pay attention now!

A life span is a flicker in the life of the universe. Any attempt at egotistical immortality is futile. We come from mystery and return to mystery. So, when some say "turn to God" it's a totally appropriate feeling-gesture.

You're Not Your Mind States

Your minds states change all the time; but, you are not any one of those mind states.

A source of the great mystery of "higher consciousness" is that there is a level "above" the ordinary everyday mind that can observe the mind. This higher level gives us the prospect of transcendence of suffering and mortality.

One could say that there is perception, mind, consciousness, and awareness. Call each of these a "level." I don't say that these levels are absolutely real and fixed; they are just general ways of mapping the vast territory which meditation explores. It does appear that each level "up" can see what's below.

Four

True goodness is like water.
Water's good for everything.
It doesn't compete ...
It goes right to the low loathsome
places,
And so finds the way

—TAO TE CHING[3]

---

3 Chapter 8, Ursula Le Guin translation

To the Core

Find a quiet place to stand. If you have a window, face the window; if outside, face the horizon.

Relax all your joints. Your finger joints, your neck, your leg joints. Let go of tension in the joints, and energy flows more freely throughout the body.

Now, imagine going to center of your bones—all the way to the marrow of your bones.

Turning Toward the Greater Light

Spending life reading spiritual texts is like living in shadows and reflections of a greater light. Turn toward the light itself.

In the past, I spent much of my life in words, in the halls of schools with students reading and reflecting off of texts. Such pursuits, however, are shadows and reflections from a greater light. True understanding is earned with silence, contemplation, prayer, and good actions.

The story is told of Nāropa, a great eleventh century Tibetan scholar who was asked by a woman, "Do you understand your words?" He responded that he did and she was happy to hear that. Then she asked, "Do you understand the meaning of your words?" He said, "Yes." She broke into tears and said, "You are a liar. My brother, a fish monger, understands the meaning of these teachings, while you don't!" That moment Nāropa began a long quest for her brother, Tilopa, followed by an even longer apprenticeship—until Nāropa realized those wisdom teachings in his heart and soul.

Our real work moves from theory to practice, and finally to realization.

Still Center

Turn, turn, turn until you're still and everything turns around you.

I turned and turned

The room was spinning
        I was spinning
Suddenly my friend said
        "Imagine that you
            are not turning
But the room is turning
around you!"

I did
Oh my! It worked
The blur of the room turning around me
        like a merry-go-round

At the Center
        my body, head, mind
became still as a rock

Yes—the universe turns
around each of us.

Toward what shall we turn?
          Toward things?
          Toward each other?
                    Or, shall we turn inward?
                    Toward dreams?
                    Toward feelings?
                              Toward God?

Turn, turn, turn
          until you're still
          and everything
          turns around you.

"Progress" in Meditation

To go for "progress" in meditation makes enlightenment a receding horizon. Effort works against us. Sit and wait. Grace may come.

This issue of progress in meditation comes up often. Students tell me that they are not making any progress at all. Meditation is not about progress—it's about giving up control and surrendering to what is. What is, is what is—both outside and inside. How can there be progress in the realm of surrender. True surrender is giving up control. So there may be no progress in the sense that the ego is controlling how things will go. If the ego must control—that is not meditation. If the ego steps aside— the very idea of progress goes away! That is meditation.

Game of Now-ness

One day I was walking home from grade school. The thought came to mind "How long can I attend to every step I take?" Suddenly, I was playing a game with myself trying to feel every step as I touched the ground. Then and there, it became obvious that the mind is easily distracted from even such a simple task. I looked at a distant spot and imagined every single step between here and there. Again and again I failed to actually accomplish that task. So began a spontaneous journey of learning how to become mindful and awake.

I shared this "game" with a friend nick-named Brave Wayne. He tried it out, but did not stay with it. Brave Wayne was the only one I shared it with. Neither my mother nor my father knew about this game. It was hard to explain, and it seemed that no one would be interested anyway. It would be many years before I shared these experiences with a very close friend devoted to meditation practice.

Self Realization Is Like Falling in Love

In my youth, I fell in love every Spring. I remember that there was always a time, a moment, before falling in love. I would feel sad and anxious in a world that had become bittersweet, filled with flowers all around, but no love in my life. A longing sense developed, and then suddenly someone caught my attention, my fancy. Days or weeks passed only thinking of her name and face. Suddenly, I was in love. Love is always there, but I had not been ready for love. The longing was like a shadow, a sign that the light of love was around the corner.

It's like that with realizing the Self. One must *long for* the Self as if falling in love. Then we are drawn from the little "self" to the wider Self—which is an expanded awareness free of identification with the objects of awareness. To fall in love with someone gets us out of the self to an expanded bigger self of two—a hint of a greater love beyond romantic love.

Listening for Silence

Meditation is like listening for Silence,
    Prayer is like talking to Silence,
    Contemplation attends to *thoughts* between Silences.
    Even deeper is bodily submission—
    To act, to dance in the space of silence.

Silence is the background of everything and nothing.

When mind becomes truly silent, thoughts stop effortlessly,
    We hear an eternal ocean within;
        Listen for it.

Life's like a dance of
    Activity, prayer, and deep silence.
Don't let the opportunity given by an opening pass by!
    The opening comes, and freedom is the choice that
    we can make,
    Not some big intentional effort.
Just allow it.
The allowing of it is the choice.
Nature and life will lead you on with many clues.
Meditation, prayer, and contemplation are helpful at such
times.

Before Practice

Before taking up a practice, we may consider reasons and goals for meditation. Maybe we want to reduce stress, to better focus in our work, to contribute to a peaceful world, or to advance our spiritual practice. Still, this is theory—goals are all theory.

We give ourselves reasons to encourage our own practice. Old habits, however, prevent us from transforming theory into action, into actual time in meditation practice. It's almost like that proverbial "leap of faith"; we just have to dive into a practice.

Later, practice takes root so deeply that we actually forget that we are doing practice. It's effortless. In this meditation-mind, cause and effect drop away and we experience the flow of all things, "isness." Theory is no longer needed. We are in *realization-action*. Practice is now life.

Training the Mind

Be still from two to five times everyday. Train the mind in peace.

Shortly after graduation, I applied for a teaching position at Sonoma State College. I felt uncertain before the interview. I was reading about meditation, but had yet to actually **do it**. Suddenly, I took the plunge. I repeated an inner mantra (a short meditation phrase) for fifteen minutes, and then looked around the room. I was calm and quiet. At the interview I was calm, centered, and made real human contact. Soon they offered me the job. That set me on the lifelong path of meditation practice.

Layers of Knowing

There are several layers of knowing that can be "named," but these names are approximations.

Our own minds are too deep, mysterious, and obtuse to be ever fully described. We can, however, imagine layers of knowing to be somewhat like:

- ◆ Awareness
- ◆ Consciousness
- ◆ Mind
- ◆ Perception
- ◆ Sense organs
- ◆ Objects (out "there" and in "here")

Don't take these categories or layers too seriously. Next, we can imagine relationships between "awareness" and "consciousness," and I do so at times—but don't take these descriptions too seriously.

Please look for yourself, so that you may find your own way toward awakening to life.

Breathe into Here-ness Now

Breathing deeply with a deep sense of the here-ness of now is instant meditation. We can do this anywhere, anytime.

While talking on the phone with a friend, I said, "Breathe deeply feeling our here-ness now." Our language is impoverished when speaking of consciousness. Here-ness is always with us; but if unawake to THAT which is right now, right here, we miss the majesty of life.

I'm writing to you (and reminding myself right NOW) to actually DO what is written about here. Right now: breathe deeply and feel the here-ness of now. Take five deep breaths, down into the lower abdomen. Relax into the here-ness of now.

Freestyle Meditation

All day long, look for moments of stillness.

Begin any time during the day with the intention "I shall look for the next gap, the next open moment when I can drop into meditation." Visualize finding at least five such gaps during the day. The times will vary from day to day. This way of finding meditation time is suitable for many people with complex lives that don't fit traditional fixed routines.

These daily meditation openings/gaps can run from a few seconds to fifteen minutes. Over time, it will feel so good that you will often create the moment for meditation because it is so charming and filled with the potential for making the rest of life more connected to love, compassion, peace, and awareness of all-that-is.

Five

Water the root, enjoy the fruit.

—MAHARISHI MAHESH YOGI

Take a Deep Break

Today, imagine taking a deep break—even from meditation. Don't meditate. Just be. Relax into what is, even if it is a "distraction"—awareness may come.

In practice, training, and learning it's easy to think that we have to keep doing the same thing over and over "no matter what." So students decide to do only the same meditation technique day after day—even with no sense of progress. In the same way many prepare for exams just going over the same material hour after hour. Patterns become calcified; there's a sense of hitting a wall over and over again. It may be time to "give up," to take a deep break—allowing the subconscious to do the work.

Walk away from the practice for a day, even longer. You'll get fresh views of the world. Meditation is vital. It will call you back again. When you start again, you'll have deeper appreciation of your practice. Some points of resistance will be gone. Buddha's final enlightenment happened after he gave up. He had some food, had some rest; discovered a moderate approach to practice. Then he became "Buddha"—awakened.

It's a Blessing

It's a blessing when someone asks you about meditation; it supports your own meditation.

A meditation question is a gift. It turns our focus to the fundamental nature of our consciousness. It humbles us because so much is at stake. Answer carefully from the depths of your heart. Admit what you don't know. Thank the questioner, for they have compelled you to return to meditation in that moment. Only in meditation, can a question about meditation be answered.

Stopping the World

Once a day
sit
until
the
world
stops.

Stay relaxed,
But firm.
You will last longer.

Forgetting the past, forgetting the future—only this
Now.
This moment contains all,
Dropping away worry—I live abundantly.

Every moment
is first and last.

Live now
and the "now" will follow you
all the days of your life.

Hear Yourself!

All day, or for just one hour: no radio, no television, no computer, no phone, no reading. Stay with yourself. Hear yourself! Much will be learned.

It's normal, natural to want to be entertained. We're all like children. We want to be distracted from ourselves. Our "self" in the sense of the small self, the ego, engages in a painful struggle against a hostile world. Call it reality. It wants to withdraw from the battle. Listening to the news on the radio; or, watching "reality television" (where we tune into the lives of other "real" people) gives us relief from ourselves. We also keep going to our computers or phones to be thrown outward to somewhere outside our little self.

I'm not saying that radio, television, computers, phone, and books are bad—I'm saying that to use these to escape deprives us of the precious opportunity to come closer to our big Self—the ground of our consciousness, which is also everyone else's consciousness. This is the ultimate reality experience. Life is short; we have no time to waste. *Be all you can be. Be here now.* Afterwards, take a break; turn on the radio, TV, computer. Remember to come back again to your Self, again and again.

Being Is ...

There is an aspect of ourselves that some call absolute reality, this is Being.

Being is ...
That feeling in your gut
That wordless power
Displacing ordinary mind
Overtaking you like the
Bright noonday sun

Being is ...
A vast space of stillness
A child crying for her mother
A city pounding with cars
Trains, footsteps, escalators, elevators

Being is everything and nothing
          A paradoxical wholeness
Absolute and Relative united
Indescribable in its totality

Standing Before the Source

Most of the noise in my life comes from my own mind.

Attending to awareness
        rather than the objects of awareness
        leads to liberation from bondage
                to objects, desires, and obsessions

Attention on awareness leads to awareness independent of objects
        Awareness becomes its own object
        It's an opening to oneness

Be open to mystery
        Stand before the Source
        Walk with the Source
        Listen to the Source
At first it is like useless silence
        But with time and practice
        comes power, love, and joy

The source is our best friend
        Leading us from "little self" to big Self

Encounters with "the Great Silence"

Much of my mystical life opened by way of silence.

One of my first encounters with "the great silence" came at age thirteen, after my first confession in a Catholic Church, right after recounting the details of disturbing actions and thoughts in my life to the priest in the confessional box. The priest said, "You are forgiven." He gave me a penance—which was to recite a couple of prayers to myself in the church pews before going home. As I performed those prayers, a profound silence came to me—deep peace and a glowing light all around. That event is still present, as if it happened only yesterday.

Much of my mystical life opened through the doorway of silence. Silence provides a **gap** in thoughts that allows entry to a reality far larger, far more awesome than what is given in the daily grind of thoughts and tasks.

Over time, I learned that many people in many cultures, in many religions, and non-religious contexts—all have had encounters with this great silence.

Space of Silence

Be still, and know that I am God!

—Psalms 46:10

Meditation is like listening for Silence
Prayer is like talking to Silence
Contemplation attends to thoughts between Silence

Dance in the space of silence

When mind becomes truly silent, thoughts stop effortlessly
We hear an eternal ocean within
Listen for it

Life's like a dance of
Activity, prayer, and deep silence

Listen

Take a few minutes to sit and listen, just listen.

Find a quiet place
where you will be undisturbed
where you feel safe
good, relaxed, and balanced

For twenty minutes
    sit and listen

Listen all around and within
    listen deeply
    stay with the act of listening

Let go of everything else
    let go of thoughts
    let go of images
    let go of desires
Just listen
    Listen
    Listen

Pray Continually

For some, continual prayer brings great peace of mind.

Paul wrote, "Rejoice always, pray without ceasing, give thanks in all circumstances ..."[4] Saint Paul suggests what is called the Prayer of Jesus (The constant repetition all day long of the phrase "Lord Jesus Christ, have mercy on me.") Those devoted to this practice report a deep inner joy by giving the mind over to this simple prayer—done all day long as one goes about daily life. Hindus and Buddhists do the same when they practice repeating a "mantra"—a spiritual phrase repeated internally all day long.

---

4 Bible, 1 Thessalonians 5:16-18.

Moment's Delight

Delight in this Moment until time is transcended.

Wherever you are now; stand in this moment now. Watch the way this moment changes in quality as you stand within it. At some point the quality of *now* changes to the bliss of existence itself.

Cultivate Spiritual Eyes

Clearly, "we" are all one. By cultivating spiritual eyes we see this.

We are all born with awesome spiritual power. But we cannot "see" it as we get older because our innocent childlike spiritual eyes have become material eyes. So we see things, see the world's tangibles; but don't see the light pervading creation. Through meditation, prayer, contemplation, study, and surrender to totality; our spiritual sight becomes stronger. We begin to see below the surface glitter of life.

Six

I am concentrated into one;
He is divided into ten.
I am ten to his one;
Many against his few.

—SUN TZU[5]

---

5 *Art of War. From "Empty and Full".* John Minford translation.

To "Hear Yourself,"
Go Deep Inside

To "hear yourself," go deep inside—not always a pretty sight. Often we find a confused tangle of thoughts, feelings, and images. Begin here.

When you first begin hearing yourself, it's a cacophony of memories and worries. What exactly do we hear when we listen to ourselves? Old songs, fears, desires, day dreams, pains in the body, sounds outside, and so much more!

Many new meditators don't deal with this "manure of experience," as Chögyam Trungpa called it. Don't throw it away. It's where we start; it's the reason why we are doing this work. From this manure comes awakening and the flower of enlightenment.

This confused mental tangle is the manure, the opportunity for transformation by way of patience and self overcoming. Look within, stay with it, and let it go.

Know Thyself ...
Take a Retreat

The family was away, and I had a little time off from work. I decided to do a four day home-based retreat. This meant spending most of that time alone.

There was plenty to do: reflecting on myself by staring out the window for an hour or two; sitting in formal meditation practice one to three times a day; listening to my own mind while walking around; being mindful while washing dishes and putting things away; occasionally talking on the phone or doing email, watching how I feel after these interactions.

A retreat is a time to gather up one's self back toward the Self. A time to rediscover one's self as one's own best friend and loving critic—a time to "know thyself."

Look at Yourself

Stop and look with total honesty at yourself—without self-judgment for or against anything.

Look at yourself. Sit there and look at yourself with total honesty – without self-judgment for or against anything. Allow an honest look at what is "you." Know thyself! This is meditation. See everything. See the real, unreal, the loves, the hates, and the neglected items. Don't pass over anything. Take it all in. Don't run away from it. Stay here.

Eventually, you see past the false "you" as the mind waves come and go. At the bottom of yourself, you find the pearl of unconditional truth. It's deeper than memories—deeper than the story of this lifetime.

Perfect Action

A perfect action is done without attachment to results. It is action aligned to your life purpose.

Do meditation as an action only for its own sake. The time you spend in meditation makes it easier for you to live your life purpose, which is expressed in specific, precise ways at each moment of presence here and now. Don't worry about results— the results take care of themselves.

Doing Not-doing

There's the reality and power of doing nothing.

"Over and over Lao Tzu says *wei wu wei*: Do not do. Doing not-doing. To act without acting, action by inaction. You do nothing yet it gets done ..."[6]

It's like flowing down a river toward the ocean. You don't have to do anything to get to the ocean. Any action taken is already taking you to the ocean. Worry adds nothing. Action without forcing would make our life deeper and more blissful. For example, I am writing this section in a state of *doing not-doing* by letting words come as they will to this page; knowing that I can keep changing and editing the page until it shapes up into its final, "perfect" form.

Many of our actions are forced; as if we're driving on a freeway while running out of gas and feeling as if the car is powered by the force of worry in our stomachs. This is silly; the car will move as long as there's gas. Stomach worry power adds no extra travel miles—unless we make better use of our gasoline. We'll

6   Comment by Ursula K. Le Guin to Chapter 3, *Tao Te Ching*.

get more miles out of that last gallon by combinations of conscious gear shifting, taking advantage of downhill slopes to use gravity rather than gasoline, slower accelerations, and so forth. With less forcing of the engine we get a longer drive to that last gas station before night comes. That's the "doing not-doing" of driving. The same applies to the rest of life and mind.

Showing Up

You're already here
        But hardly know it.

Every day, a flood of
        phone calls
        memories
television
        radio
        newspapers
family, friends, coworkers
all demanding attention.

Your mind spins with
fantasies
        visions
        dreams.

From dreams and vision
New worlds begin.

The greatest vision is to imagine a life lived here-and-now.

So now!
Show up for your own life.
You'll be glad you did.

The sweepstakes ticket says, "Must be present to win."

A friend in the acting business was going to an audition. She said, "Showing up is half the job."

Arriving

Sometimes I begin classes by asking students to "arrive." Everyone is rushing to make it on time, over and over each day. You can see the anxiety on their faces. Some are constantly studying for other classes while they are in my class. They are not where they are.

So, I ask them to be still and quiet for a minute or two—so that we all can arrive together to the same spot.

Between Body and Spirit

We may find ourselves at different points between the axis of the body and spirit. Enlightenment could be seen as a balance point between the extremes of body and spirit. But, it's not quite like that either!

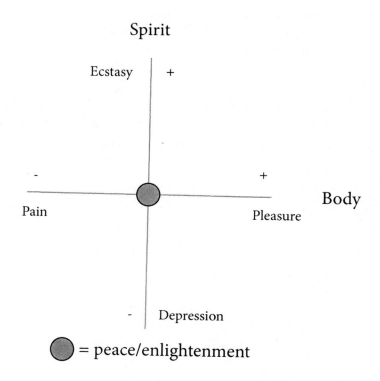

One Pointed

Attend
        to one point of focus
        for a few seconds
Do it again
        do it again
Stay one-pointed in emptiness
        The mind becomes empty and luminous
Become one with your own life

My father would say "Watch your step!" in English, although he mostly spoke Portuguese. He was really trying hard to make his point. It was an injunction to be mindful.

Effortless Desire

We effortlessly desire truth, beauty, and wisdom; souls are made of truth, beauty, and wisdom.

Walk Softly

Walk softly, mindfully upon this earth. Be mindful of the impact of everything consumed. The earth is a precious jewel.

To be aware of the earth below our feet and the sky above our head is the beginning of loving the earth. It is that simple. We start killing fewer animals because we feel their feelings—even insects begin to get respect as sensitive beings. We begin turning off lights more often as we see the connection between consuming carbon based electricity and the destruction of the earth. In other words: we begin to clean up after ourselves as we walk around; we don't wait to come back "later." After all, later never comes. Walking softly happens this moment, right now.

Meditate Often Everyday

If you meditate more than once a day, you can look back on the day's meditations as a unified whole. Life becomes steady.

Today: Meditate five times, ten minutes each time. Do it at odd times when there is a sense of a gap between daily activities.

Seven

When humor and spaciousness
are present,
Meditation arises effortlessly.

—SOGYAL RINPOCHE[7]

Who says my poems are poems?
My poems are not poems.
After you know my poems
are not poems,
Then we can begin to discuss poetry!

—RYŌKAN[8]

7 *The Tibetan Book of Living and Dying.*

8 *One Robe, One Bowl: The Zen Poetry of Rōykan.*

Early Awakening

Awaken early in the morning
Before the light of dawn.

While still in bed, think:
I shall get up and take
a quiet walk outside.
Just following my footsteps
being silent within,
Aware of space around,
Aware of space within.

Get dressed; go outside.
Feel the body and mind awaken,
Feel the texture of emotions stirring,
            Feel the totality of being-here-now.

When you walk, just walk,
Aware of what's passing by
Within the mind, around the body;
            Intensely feel being-here-now.

You may think

You should be solving problems,
You should be planning.
You are! Already!
You are contacting
the subterranean powers
of your own being.

"Little Self" Hides the "Big Self"

The "little self" hides the "big Self" which was and is always here-and-now. So there's nothing to do. Take the position. Breathe and wait.

The grand purpose of the humble practice of meditation is to strip away the little self long enough so that the big Self is revealed. There is a timeless tradition in the East that makes this quite clear. Perhaps as long as 3,000 years ago, in *The Yoga Sutras*, Patanjali wrote,

> Yoga is the settling of the mind into silence.

> When the mind has settled, we are established in our essential nature, which is unbounded consciousness.

> Our essential nature is usually overshadowed by the activity of the mind.[9]

The big Self as our **unbounded consciousness** is already, always with us—but is covered up by all the thought waves. It's like the ocean. If we only look at the waves on the surface, we miss all the depth and wonder of the ocean below. To meditate is to dive below the waves and go deep into the vastness that is below.

9 Chapter 1, Sutras 2, 3, and 4.

Frustration Tells Us "I am not this, I am not that ..."

Frustration is telling us that ego is not real. Frustration, discomfort, and pain tell us "I am not this, I am not that ..."

It's almost too easy when everything is "going right." We can easily talk ourselves into thinking that we are so "enlightened," that we have found the right way to be. We may even go about showing other people the right way to be—because we are happy, contented, and successful. But, reality is ever tricking us. Suddenly, something changes. Suddenly there is pain, discomfort, and frustration. We're not so sure any more. Our ego may come up with all kinds of strategies for holding its fortress together. After all, once we have "it," we must not let go! Here is the greatest illusion.

If our innate nature is spacious as the sky, we cannot be "this" or "that." We are free. But, the ego needs to say, "I am rich. I am good. I am ..." It fixes, makes permanent that which is not lasting. It holds in place that which cannot be held. Meditation helps us to acknowledge frustration, discomfort, and pain in life. It's not something to be judged or denied. It just is. Be with it until it lets go, or doesn't let go. Work with it to come to a more precise, clear, and spacious view. Later, a new sense of thankfulness arises. The humbling message of reality in the form of frustration, discomfort, and pain has done its work to pierce the veil cast by ego.

Postponed Intentions

*Oh! I'll do my practice after I do _____ (fill in the blank).
Soon you forget, and a day passes. No practice.*

The best of intentions are forgotten in an instant. "Oh! Not yet. I'll practice after washing the dishes." The dishes get washed, then the phone rings, then you turn on the computer to send an email, ten emails later, it's dinner time. The day passes. You go to bed thinking, "I'll practice after I wake up, before anything else happens."

So it goes. The excuses mount. A lifetime passes. Maybe in the next lifetime ...

Impulses Come and Go

During meditation practice, impulses come and go. If at all possible, resist these impulses until practice time is over. That's what makes it practice.

Sometimes we sit and suddenly forget our practice. We get up and do something. That is being overwhelmed by an impulse—thought turned into action (when we were practicing non-action). An impulse is stronger than a thought—it's more like a twitch, a sudden sense of movement toward some object.

During practice you may feel an impulse to get up and do something. Don't resist; don't act; let it pass by. That's the essence of practice. Impulses come and go independent of whether or not they're acted upon. Impulses to start writing down notes in the calendar will come and go. Impulses to go to the bathroom come and go. While in practice mode; don't act, don't feed impulses. In that moment of non-action we get closer to the root of all our desires and impulses. There are layers of impulses from gross to subtle. The impulse to get up and move is a gross level example; the impulse to solve a problem is a subtle level example.

These impulses may be useful reminders of what we need to do for our day; they may be creative insights that come to us during meditation; in which case, they're gifts. Realize what it is. Let it go. It will be available later as needed. Now is now. Relax again in what is, as-it-is.

Standing Below

Understanding—"to stand under"
        Below the surface
        To see what usually goes unnoticed

Light is noticed
        When too bright or too dim
        At such times we "see the light"

Look around a room
        What's hidden is the light
        A clearing and opening around and
        within us

A room is an opening
        A nothingness, void, space
        Allowing objects to be there
        Light itself needs no place
        It pervades even empty space

Understanding unfolds being
        Objects-at-hand present themselves
        Before us and within us
We are here!
        Standing free

Appointments with the Self

We easily make appointments, but fail to make the most important daily appointments with the Self.

I meditate two or three times a day: in the morning, afternoon, and evening—between ten and twenty minutes each period. At first it seemed impossible. But it's easy—if you know the secret. Appointments with yourself are as important as appointments with others. The benefits are a steady clearer mind, a greater ability to concentrate, peace of mind, and greater overall happiness. These benefits spill over into better health, compassion for others, and a sense of successful living.

Give Us this Day, Our Daily Practice

The power and value of daily practice is awesome. It's the work we do to refine ourselves, like polishing a very hard stone.

Habits from this life and our heritage are really difficult to change. It requires work or labor—like learning to play a musical instrument. In the beginning progress is easy, but it takes years of practice, attention, and help from those farther along to actually master the instrument, to release its full potential for making music—and to enter a musical tradition.

Practice is directed toward harmony and balance, toward perception and understanding, toward the ability to handle life without "freaking out." Eventually a sense of humor arises about our own inability to stay with it. We may fall again and again, just to get back up. "Getting back up" becomes the practice. That's the nature of practice: to make mistakes, shrug them off, and try again. A piece of music is learned by making thousands of mistakes. By listening to those mistakes over time, you eliminate them until the piece of music is perfected. Once the piece is perfected, it may still be just a technical perfection because there is another stage in which one learns how to express one's own feelings through that piece of music. It's no longer just yourself, but a new self that is part of the instrument and the tradition of music you are living within. Spiritual practice is much the same.

Humor in Everything

Children see humor in everything
Tension upon tension released into laughter
They wiggle, they sing, they make up rhymes,
draw and paint, write and paste paper to paper and
themselves!

When we become narcissistic, self-conscious,
worried about doing right, problem-focused
We have a real problem:
being way too serious adults!

Jesus said "… unless you change and
become like little children …"[10]

Laugh and be adults living with mystery and
ignorance
With childhood intensity
Like Merlyn,
   Becoming younger with the passing years.

10 Bible, Matthew 18:3

Who Is the "Self?"

Who is "self?" Who is "other"? Look deeply enough and we find that it's true—"We are one!" Yes, the same Self everywhere.

Spiritual work begins to shrink the "self" to nothing; but the "Self," the big Self, expands toward all-that-is. That Self, is the Self of all, the Self of the World; eventually we awaken to seeing, hearing, and feeling the oneness-of-all.

Ordinary Life Is Extraordinary

Ordinary life is extraordinary—if we awaken to the luminosity of this moment.

Every moment is special, is extraordinary; but, we must have "eyes to see." There is beauty and charm in spiritual work—which is to climb the mountain of awareness until our vision is panoramic.

Peace of Mind

Peace of mind comes with "no effort" at all. That's surrender. Struggle for peace of mind undercuts peace of mind. But don't be lazy!

We can't make our minds peaceful. Yes, there is effort in invoking the meditation moment, the nonviolent moment of the heart, mind, and soul. The movement into peace happens—peace is not the work of the ego, or little self; it's of Grace.

Eight

Once upon a time, I, Chuang Tsu,
dreamed I was a butterfly flying
happily here and there,
enjoying life without knowing who I
was.
Suddenly I woke up and I was indeed
Chuang Tsu.
Did Chuang Tsu dream he was a
butterfly,
or did the butterfly dream he was
Chuang Tsu?

—CHUANG TSU[11]

11 *Inner Chapters*

You Are the World

The world comes into existence when you are awake and goes out of existence when you sleep. You are the world!

During sleep you live in a world of dreams, and sometimes utter quiet. Of these two states, the dream world is most like waking life. The quiet state is beyond the world altogether. Is not life itself, when recalled (as memories) like a dream? A dreamer sometimes realizes they are in a dream, and thereby breaks the power of the dream.

Coming and Going

Everything comes and goes. We cannot stop this changing turning world.

Our thoughts, too, are like the world—coming and going. Only abiding awareness is real. Before the ocean of *being-awareness* all arrives and passes away; yet, that ocean remains. The final step—let go of the thought of "being-awareness." Let go of the thought of "enlightenment." Let it go into trust and surrender. That is peace.

Completely Let Go

Completely let go. Letting go leads to deep healing. Completely let go three to five times a day.

Today, try doing the following:

1. Completely let go of everything. Be like a "blob." Deeply relaxed.

2. Breath deeply. Long enough to activate a stronger sense of life energy.

3. Proceed back into action, doing what you need to be doing.

4. As the day proceeds completely let go again. Do as many as five sessions of completely letting go.

Teaching and Teachers

Listen to teachers while listening to your inner teacher.

Along the spiritual path there are many teachers; many seekers of truth and wisdom get addicted to listening to many teachers, many teachings. Eventually, they get confused; never finding what they seek; not even knowing what they seek.

When searching for a teacher or teachings, look from the perspective of your true inner teacher; your Self. This is rare and difficult. It will take time.

Twelve Seconds

Take short mind breaks together.

Take short mind breaks with a friend.
        It's like going to the gym;
        We could exercise at home,
        But it's too easy to be lax.
        At the gym, others keep us on track.
        We need a spiritual gym too!

A simple mutual support practice developed with a close friend:
        One of us calls the other;
        We talk about our states of mind.
        One of us says "twelve seconds?"
        The other usually says "Yes!"

Concentrate on whatever you wish—
        A word, a thought, the tip of the finger,
        The wall, a clock,
        Your breath.
        Anchor your mind on that one thing for
        twelve seconds;

You will be fortunate if one-pointed
For only one second!

As our minds become a little more open, peaceful,
quiet,
Work becomes a little more focused,
productive, and fulfilling.

Actual stillness is less important
Than what we learn about our mind
state.
Is our mind filled with anxiety?
Is it driven toward some objective?
Are we too serious?

To know your mind is
a leap forward into awakening.

Stay with the Real

Everyday
so many things compete for your attention.
If you try to keep up with all of them
        you will go mad.

        Stay with what is real—
        The real that is simple and whole.

Distraction

At the end of many meditations, I know, I have not stayed focused on the practice. There was distraction.

Yet, upon coming back out, the world seems new again, is filled with more energy. I'm more in contact with the fuller resources of creation.

Even distraction helps us. Just become aware that it's distraction.

Stages

First—you've got to show up
With your body, heart, and soul

Second—practice staying in the present
With the many techniques
To anchor you in the present
Or, make up your own techniques
To "trick" yourself into being here

Third—practice, practice, practice
          until it's no longer practice
But natural, free, and easy

Fourth—practice listening
          until you arrive at the still point
Of the swirling world

Fifth—speak and "walk the talk"

Sixth—expect no results

Seventh—go back to work
Back to your friends

Love them by being
Steady in your realization

Eighth—just Be
        Stay realized
        Live the truth

Swirls of Stories

Life is "the unfinished story that ends with eternity."[12]

Storytelling is the oldest medium,
      Stories repeated over time and place
      By one storyteller after another.

      Media offers images of images;
      Life becomes a story lived elsewhere.

      We spend time gazing at
      Imaginary worlds on interactive screens;

      Television, radio, cellular phones, the Internet
      are Worldmakers,
      Worldweavers,
      Dream machines.

      Maybe it's better this way,
            The stories outlast us;
      "Someday I'll just be a re-run!"

      Are not our minds
            Story tellers too?

12 From a poem by Diane Shavelson, 2007.

Apply Attention

All life is meditation if you apply attention to each moment as you live through it.

We move between focus and distraction. Most of our lives are lived in distraction, attention darting here and there. Without focus, our lives become scattered and lacking in purpose. Little gets accomplished, or we do not accomplish that which we feel is most important. We miss fully experiencing our life in each moment. And, we do not clearly put our attention on determining our goals, or what we are doing toward accomplishing them right now.

Meditation focuses the mind on one point, here-and-now. And with that focus, every moment opens into a life fully lived. So apply attention to what's here now! Gently, remain here and now ...

Be Finite, Find Infinity

Within our finiteness, we find the window to infinity.

This is the great paradox of life; that to come to God we must submit, surrender to God. At that moment, God lifts us up.

Drop the Props

Don't get stuck on props such as beads, incense, bells, or alter images. Use them only as anchors; they are not the path, nor goal itself.

Nothing more need be said.

Nine

We shall not cease from exploration,
And the end of all our exploring
Will be to arrive where we started
And know the place for the first
time.

—T. S. Eliot[13]

13 *Four Quartets, "Little Gidding"*

You Give the World Meaning

You are outside the world, even while living in the world. You give the world meaning.

Watching yourself is your first step toward overcoming the world. Eventually, you get to know yourself as if you are your own best friend in the world. Watch the world; and, watch yourself in or out of the world. Step back just enough to understand your own reaction patterns in the world. But, don't step back so much so as to disengage from life. True enlightenment, fulfillment, or salvation requires that we engage in life. For that is how we express and receive love.

Look Around

Look around slowly. See, hear, feel all the details of the immediate environment here-now, without the judgment of "this is good, this is bad."

We can begin this simple practice anywhere, at anytime. Sometimes it's helpful to begin by looking out the window and allowing the mind to slow down, and maybe even stop thinking; just looking, gazing slowly outward. Move the head slowly around. Allow the eyes to settle spontaneously on one detail after another, without getting fixed on anything. Keep flowing around all of the space, objects and surface details; important not to be naming, categorizing, and judging what is good or bad. Let everything be where and whatever it is—in a deep wordless flow. Extend, if possible, to the senses of hearing and touch.

This practice is the simple embodiment of the idea of being-here-now. For a moment we "reach out and touch the local universe." No longer in our heads but in our world as it is.

Tourists in Our Hometown

Learning to be a tourist in our hometown returns the sense of Life that is lost in ordinary life. Intense, yet gentle, this intention is natural meditation and prayer, informing life with the wonder of this present moment.

> If Life feels dull,
> Surroundings and true Self become unnoticed.
> We desire travel
> To get away from home
> For new "angles of perception";
> For a while, things look new,
> Then dullness sets in again.
>
> Remember childhood?
> Everything was a wonder,
> Everything was fresh—
> To smell a flower, a pure joy;
> Often making playful sounds

My best friend and I walked through a little shop near home. The store attendant asked us, "Where are you from?" We said, "We live nearby." She was surprised and said, "You look like tourists. You seem to enjoy everything here as if for the first time."

My Religion Is Love

My grandson asked, "Grandpa, what is your religion?" Thinking deeply, deciding to be honest, I said, "My religion is love."

I said to my grandson, "My religion is love; which is what great religions teach—love." Then he said, "So which one is your religion?" Out of my mouth (and heart) came, "All of them, if they are about love." I also wanted to say that the great sages are humbled by the encounter with the mystery, the truth of that which cannot be spoken, of that union with the spirit known directly, while indescribable. That was too much to say; it says nothing anyway! My grandson wanted me to pick one religion, just like buying a car or computer; but, that's not my way.

I studied, digested, and internalized many religions; finding all leading to the same place inside myself. That is my particular spiritual non-religious perspective on religion. Spirituality is very inner, very personal—but as we share our spiritual lives we build common languages with names, texts, rituals, and symbols which become religions. Religions naturally happen everywhere; they are spiritual support groups.

One Pointed

Attend

       to one point of focus

       for a few seconds

Do it again

       do it again

Stay one-pointed in emptiness

       The mind becomes empty and luminous

Become one with your own life

World Making

We have responsibility for our corner of the Creation; an obligation to realize that we (as humans) are world makers. We do it all the time! It begins with the quality of our consciousness.

Consciousness is the ground of our being. Without consciousness, our world does not exist. The world comes into existence when we awaken and goes out of existence when we sleep. So consciousness is like the source. Our consciousness holds the image of the macrocosm (God or Universe or all-that-is). Attention is the action of shaping the open field of consciousness into form. Consciousness is the root of the universe. All knowledge, all awareness depends on consciousness. To live fully, live from consciousness.

So, as consciousness, the attention is directed toward certain desires and goals. The direction of attention is the primary act of will which moves subtle levels of energy around in the universe. How this happens, is the subject of both mysticism and physics.

As attention is directed toward an un-realized desire, the matrix of the energy of the universe is impacted. Say that a movement occurs. Does it create energy? Does it direct energy? I don't know. But, focusing energy in a certain direction begins movement of energy, which leads to movement of what seems like thought and matter.

Finally, matter is assembled until it becomes the objects all around us that are the results of attention focusing desires into objective and subjective goals.

Practice

Upon awakening, before engaging in the day's normal rounds, make yourself comfortable. Lay down in bed with a determination to stay awake. Imagine your inner voice repeating over and over again the phrase "I am." Say the inner "I" with the in breath and the inner "am" with the out breath. Do this over and over for about fifteen minutes. Then get up and begin your day's activity, informed with the peace of knowing simply that "I am." This is a basic affirmation of existence—nothing more or less.

Forget Outcomes

Krishna told Arjuna,
"You are only given your labors,
not the fruits of your labors.
Do not be attached to the results
of your labors."

Demanding, expecting
a specific future
causes suffering;
God's will is greater than
individuals, groups, nations,
the whole earth and cosmos.
The ancient Hindu scriptures say
you are only granted your work, your duty,
not the fruits of your work or duty.
Show up,
Do what is in front of you NOW,
NOW is all you have.

Awakening Within Dreams

"Row, row, row your boat, gently down the stream.
Merrily, merrily, merrily, merrily,
Life is but a dream."
—Children's Nursery Rhyme

One morning while awaking I became aware of a misty moment when I knew I was awake, yet aware of my half-asleep mind. I was amazed!

Everyday waking-life is like a dream. Life flows, experiences arise and fade. If we awaken within the dream, we step toward a mysterious freedom.

As my father's mind was slipping away, he said in Portuguese, "This was all like a dream." My mother, also in her 80's, said that her entire life was just like a dream. As years pass, the past becomes a dream—time's river taking us back to the ocean of being.

Nighttime dreams feel as real as waking life. And, don't we often walk around filled with daydreams and ideals, ruminations and plans? These are dreams-within-the-dream.

Everyday perception is like a flickering candle. Knowing this flickering dreamlike quality of life brings perspective and freedom. At last we awaken to the abiding Self!

Nothing to Do;
Nowhere to Go

There's nothing to do! Be here. Just be here now for a while.

By "doing non-doing" we reside in reality's ocean. We relax. Yes, things get done as our days unfold. Yes, planning and work still get done. For to do a "sit down strike" on life is doing violence. We must move and act. But, we don't need to force things—that is "the doing of non-doing."

Faith Mind

When we worry, it's as if being hunted down by wild tigers.

The world is uncertain; the mind generates worry. Almost all worry never comes to pass. Total certainty is impossible; therefore, *faith mind* is a great help in living with confidence.

Meditation practice may seem like so little, just like air and water seem like so little (until we don't have them). The little things, totally taken for granted, however, are the ground on which we stand. Meditation pays attention to our ground as consciousness. Nothing more; nothing less.

Basic Training

Meditation is basic training for cultivating a nonviolent world. "Self-other" are two sides of one coin.

The world needs peace and love. To have peace and love we need to intensify our awareness of the "other" so as to see ourselves from their position. We don't need commandments and rules; instead we need to sit, be still and truly see, hear, and feel the reality of who "we" really are. This is the real, experiential basis of *ahimsa* ("to not harm," "nonviolence"). We can't talk ourselves into this; there is only the way of direct realization. My lifework is to encourage others (and myself) into a life of constant meditation/awareness. This is basic training in *ahimsa*.

FURTHER READING

Suzuki, Shunryu. *Zen Mind, Beginner's Mind*. Tokyo: Weatherhill, 1999.

Trungpa, Chögyam. *Meditation in Action*. Boston: Shambhala, 2004.

Maharishi Mahesh Yogi. *Science of Being and Art of Living: Transcendental Meditation*. New York: Meridian, 1995.

Nisargadatta Maharaj. *I Am That: Talks with Sri Nisargadatta Maharaj*. Durham, North Carolina: The Acorn Press, 1988.

Rinpoche, Sogyal. *The Tibetan Book of Living and Dying*. San Francisco: HarperSanFrancisco, 1993.

Easwaran, Eknath. *Meditation: A simple 8-point program for translating spiritual ideals into daily life*. Tomales, California: Nilgiri Press, 1991.

Lao Tzu. *Tao Te Ching*. Translated by Gia-Fu Feng and Jane English. New introduction and notes by Jacob Needleman. New York: Vintage Books, 1989.

Lao Tzu. *Tao Te Ching: A Book about the Way and the Power of the Way*. Translated by Ursula K. Le Guin. Boston: Shambhala, 1998.

Bhagavad Gita. Translated by Stephen Mitchell. New York: Harmony Books, 2000.

Dhammapada: The Sayings of the Buddha. Rendering by Thomas Byrom. New York: Bell Tower, 1976.

The Upanishads. Second edition. Introduced and translated by Eknath Easwaran; Notes and afterward by Michael Nagler. Tomales, California: Nilgiri Press, 2007.

The Yoga Sutras of Patanjali. Translated by Alistair Shearer. New York: Bell Tower, 1982.

Holy Bible. New International Version. Grand Rapids: Zondervan Publishing House, 1984.

Al-Qur'ān. Contemporary translation by Ahmed Ali. Princeton: Princeton University Press, 1984.

————

The Center for Contemplative Mind in Society
http://www.contemplativemind.org/

The Meditation Infocenter in HolisticOnline.com
http://1stholistic.com/Meditation/hol_meditation.htm

Philosopher-at-Large Blog: Philosophy/Wisdom/Mediation
Written and Spoken by Americ Azevedo & Friends
http://philosopher-at-large.com/

ABOUT THE AUTHOR

Americ Azevedo is a lecturer in Peace and Conflict Studies, and Engineering, at the University of California, Berkeley. Outside academe he leads meditation groups, gives talks and facilitates dialogues on philosophical, spiritual, and technical topics.

He has taught philosophy and religion at San FranciscoState University and Dominican University of California; information systems, leadership, management, and finance at Saint Mary's College of California, Golden Gate University, University of San Francisco, and John F. Kennedy University.

His consulting career includes acting CEO during company reorganizations, development of e-learning and collaborative systems for universities and companies, website development, management consulting, and corporate training. He is co-founder and architect of the CyberCampus at Golden Gate University.

Visit Americ Azevedo's website at http://americazevedo.com.

CPSIA information can be obtained at www.ICGtesting.com
Printed in the USA
LVOW090846240812

295594LV00003B/372/P

Nanini

Meditation

Meditation: Waking Up to Life

Meditation: Waking Up To Life is a collection of spontaneous reflections on meditation and daily life. These short considerations express the flavor of the meditative experience. Meditation is different for each person. There is no right or wrong way; there is no successful or unsuccessful outcome. In fact, focusing on results is antithetical to the meditative process. I give you some of my thoughts in hopes of freeing you to come up with your own personal experience and practice. *Let go, relax. Be present. Here-and-Now. Find a moment, any moment; anywhere; any time; right now. Meditate into Life.*

"The tone of the book is so inviting, and I think it will be of great value to people who have a meditation practice, and to those who have never meditated. ... It is a call to waking up, to being fully present in each moment."
— Charles Halpern
Chair and Co-Founder, Center for Contemplative Mind in Society; Author of
Making Waves and Riding the Currents: Activism and the Practice of Wisdom

Americ Azevedo teaches at the University of California, Berkeley. He is a life-long meditator and philosopher of everyday life. In addition to his background in philosophy and world religions, he has taught and worked in computer technology, where he was a pioneer in online education and virtual communities; and in business, as a consultant specializing in company reorganizations. He has conducted "Philosophers' Forums" in the community, as well as leading meditation retreats. He currently teaches Nonviolence, Engineering Ethics, and Meditation.

www.cognella.com   800.200.3908

ISBN 978-193555103-4
9 781935 551034
SKU 70065-1